Author: Laura Knight
✉ lknight200@gmail.com

Illustrations: Aarin Stewart
✉ Aarin.Stewart@yahoo.com

Photography: Richard Salas
www.RichardSalas.com

* Additional Photography & Consultant Credits (below)

Be kind to the planet.
Be kind to each other.

VISIT US ONLINE AT:
www.FriendlyPlanet.Club

This project represents the unwavering support of numerous people. It would not have been possible without the creative collaboration of friends, artists, and photographers that share the same passion in protecting our ecosystem.

Acknowledgments, Credits, & Additional Thanks To:

Photo Credits: p. 32-34, & back cover (CC0 Public Domain) @ www.Pixabay.com

Editor: Rachael Salas ✉ rachael.salas@icloud.com

Educational Consultants: Silvia Stewart
Lindsay Lezama

Thanks to my friend, Harry Pacheco, who inspired me to self-publish. Also an author, Harry is on a mission to stop bullying. Discover his wonderful books online.

www.harryEpacheco.com

First Edition Self-Published by: Laura Knight © 2016
Newport Beach, CA

Printed in China.   Distributed in the U.S.

Text copyright © 2013 by Laura Knight.
Illustrations copyright © 2013 by Aarin Stewart.
Photography copyright © 2012 by Richard Salas.

All rights reserved.

ISBN 978-0-692-80525-1

All Rights Reserved. No part of this publication may be reproduced, stored in a retrieval system, or transmitted in any form or by any means, electronic, mechanical, photocopying, recording, or otherwise, without written permission of the publisher and all parties involved.

Illustrator & Photographers retain ownership to their work, with copyright to reproduce their own images in any form.

Fonts: KG Red Hands & Janda Manatee @http://kimberlygeswein.com

PLEASE NOTE: *Do not feed, touch, or disturb wildlife. Children must be supervised at all times.*

Dedicated to the children who will grow up to protect our oceans.

FUN FACTS

Guadalupe fur seals spend most of their lives out at sea. Their furry coat keeps them warm under water.

FUN FACTS

Most fish swim together in groups called schools to avoid being eaten by predators!

FUN FACTS

*Most of our planet is covered by water.
The oceans are so big, it is hard for scientists to explore them all.*

We dove deep into the water, using our front flippers to pick up speed.

It was a race to the finish, as I continued to lead.

FUN FACTS

Animal life can be found at all depths of the ocean, from the surface to the deepest trenches that are over seven miles below the surface.

FUN FACTS

An octopus has eight arms and three hearts.
It has a good memory and is considered to be very smart.

FUN FACTS

The hammerhead shark's unusual-shaped head with the eyes positioned far to the sides give the shark unique binocular vision to hunt for food.

FUN FACTS

Trash left behind can be very dangerous to the ocean animals. Many animals face extinction because of pollution.

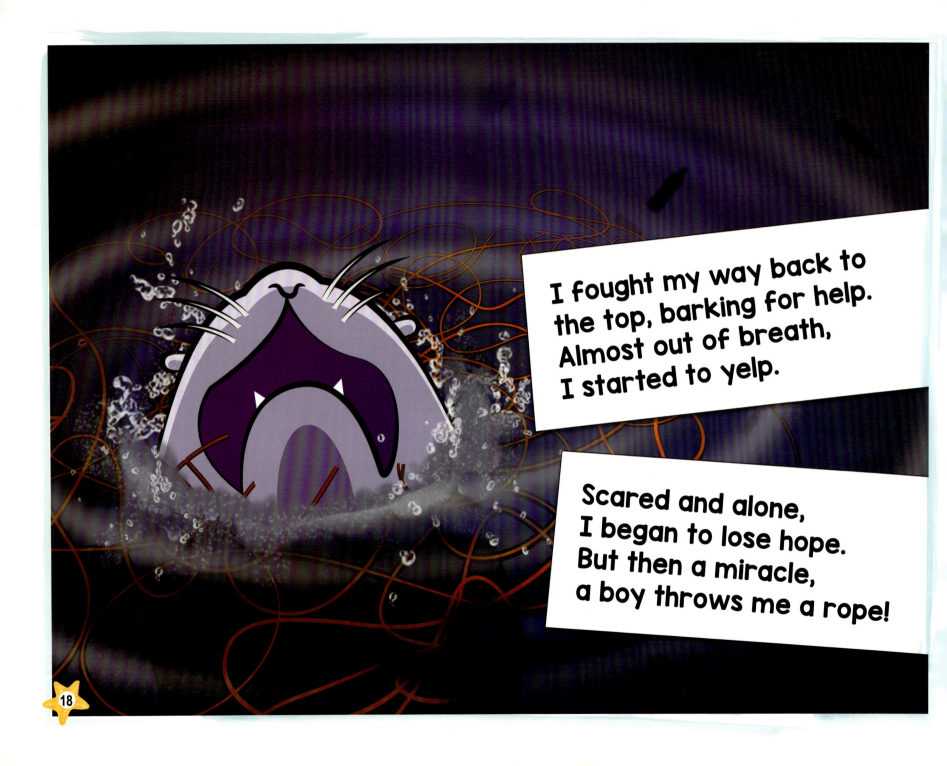

High up above,
sat a special red boat.

It came to my rescue and
I was pulled onto a float.

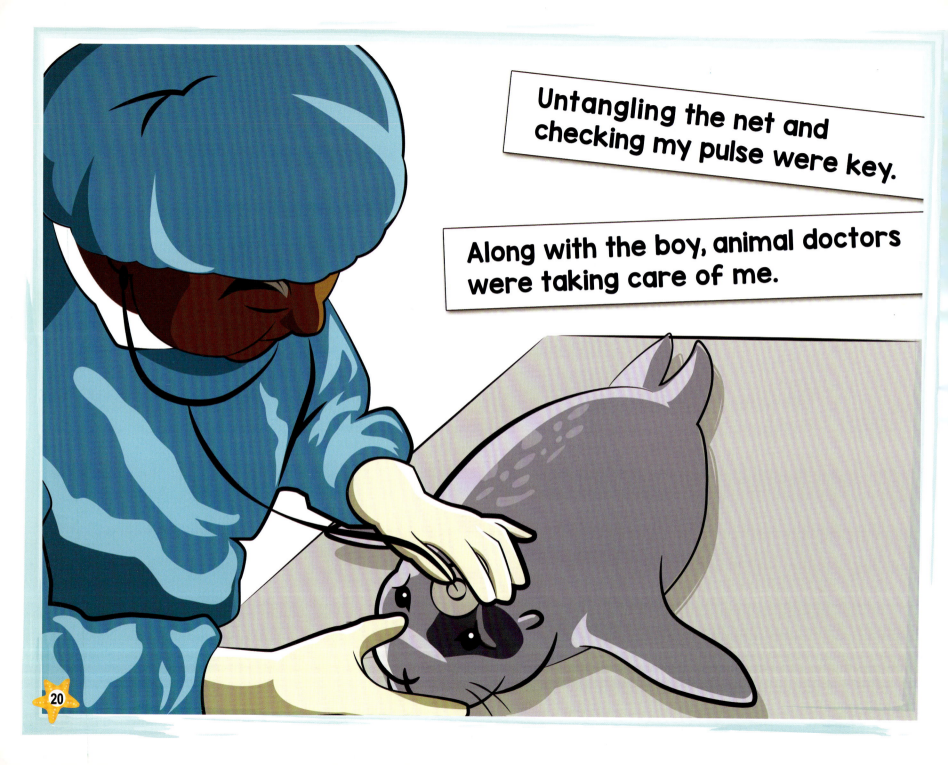

The boy, Charlie, would visit me every day. He kept me company while I was away.

He said he was sorry that some humans pollute the big blue sea.

He knew **all life** on earth was important, even for you and me.

FUN FACTS

Sea turtles are hatched from an egg on land, but they usually spend their entire life at sea. Many sea turtle species are considered endangered.

FUN FACTS

Sea lions, seals, and walruses are part of the same marine mammal family. These sea lions play together and sound like barking dogs.

Sometimes help comes from unexpected faces, but that's what makes the world connect in all sorts of places.

FUN FACTS

The whale shark is the largest fish on the planet.
They can grow up to 46 feet in length. That is longer than a school bus!

Be responsible and pick-up trash left behind.

So, Earth will be safer for all of its kind.

FUN FACTS

Seahorses are named for the shape of their head, which looks like the head of a tiny horse. A baby seahorse is about the size of a jelly bean.

FUN FACTS

Kids can do a lot to protect the ocean, like picking up trash and making sure plastic bottles and bags never get in the ocean. You can make a BIG difference!

Help Kids to MAKE CONNECTIONS & ASK QUESTIONS

LISTENING COMPREHENSION

Respond to Literature: Have the child share their favorite part of the story. The objective is to remind the child that stories have a structure, a way in which the things in them happen. For example, stories have a beginning, middle, and end.

Make Predictions (Oral Language)
Tell the child that sometimes they can use the information in the story to think about what might happen next.
- Reread page 14. Spot mentions he was under attack.

Ask: *Do you think a hungry shark could have attacked Spot?*
Ask: *Why is the trash in the ocean dangerous to ocean animals?*

Learning Lessons (Oral Language)
Ask: *Why is it important to throw away our trash?*
Ask: *What is pollution? What does it mean to recycle?*

Activity: Sandbox Discovery

Materials needed: Sandbox or Water Table, sea shells, candy wrapper, crayon, straw, plastic bag, empty water bottle or can, facial tissue, crumpled paper, small toy, and a slice of bread.
- Ask the child to pretend he/she is at the beach. Hide a few items somewhat buried in the sand and work together to determine which things belong.

Explain to the child what is considered: trash, recyclable, or reusable.

DEVELOP COMPREHENSION

Identify Setting: Have the child explain where the story takes place.

Relate to Personal Experiences (Oral Language)
Ask: *Have you ever been to the beach? What did you see?*

Activity: Field Trip

- Under adult supervision, take the opportunity to explore your local park, beach, or marine center.
- Discuss what animals or insects live in the environment. Observe the setting together.

Ask: *How do animals survive? Where do they live? What kind of food do they eat?*

MAKING CONNECTIONS

Discuss the characteristics of the ocean & the ocean animals

<u>Build A Robust Vocabulary (Oral Language)</u>
- Have the child talk about and *describe* the animals and the ocean environment in the story. **Define Vocabulary:** *large, small, fast, fury, cold, red, etc.*

🛟 **Activity: Introduce Words**
- Reread page 29. Use a jelly bean or paper clip to help the child visualize the size of a seahorse

Ask: *Which ocean animal in this book is the largest?* (Reread page 27)

<u>Relate To Environment (Oral Language)</u>
- Find objects in the room to describe their size or color or texture

AUTHOR'S PURPOSE

Discuss the theme: Helping each other.
Ask: *Who helped rescue Spot the sea pup from getting hurt?*
Ask: *How did Spot get better?*

<u>Relate To Personal Experiences (Oral Language & Access Prior Knowledge)</u>
- Have the child talk about a time someone helped them or they helped someone else.
- Have the child name family members or relatives, such as a grandparent or aunt. Prompt child to share information about an event in which this happened.

Ask (example): *Does someone help you, when you get sick?*

🛟 **Creative Activity: Friendly Planet (Collage)**
- Ask the child to observe when friends or family help each other. Then have them make drawings on globe-shaped green and blue construction paper to illustrate the act of kindness. Collect & build a collage of these memories to create a "Friendly Planet". Help write a short caption on each piece of art.
[Classroom Tip: Paper plates make a great circular canvas for children's drawings.]

Visit website for additional resources: **www.FriendlyPlanet.Club**

Author's inspiration to write about Spot!

Laura Knight
Author

The art of storytelling has always been a passion of mine. I hope to inspire children to "be your best" through heroic and unforgettable characters. I am also a surfer living in California, which has greatly encouraged my efforts to protect our ocean. This is my first self-published book and it would not have been possible to create without the contribution of these two talented and amazing friends!

Be kind to the planet.
Be kind to each other.

Richard Salas
Photographer

is a California native and graduate from Brooks Institute of Photography, where he was mentored by Ernest Brooks II and first introduced to diving and underwater photography. Richard has worked professionally in digital media for over twenty-four years and his unique approach to bringing out the texture and depth of his underwater subjects is informed by years of experience in lighting products and people. He has authored three books of photography, including *Sea of Light, Underwater Photography of California's Channel Islands*, *Blue Visions, Underwater Photography from the Mexican Border to the Equator* and *Luminous Sea, Underwater Photography from Washington to Alaska*. Richard's mission is to take the viewer through a marine biosphere where humanity's impact is an undeniable force. While many new endemic species are discovered every year, others have disappeared from it completely. The striking power of Richard's images radiates the light of unique vitality that resides in every organism he encounters. He teaches underwater photography in Alaska, Canada, California and Mexico and is a strong advocate for the sea and it's inhabitants.

www.RichardSalas.com

Aarin Stewart
Illustrator

Dedicated to the arts, I have been drawing pictures since I can remember. As an avid supporter for the National Center for Science and Civic Engagement, I seek ways I can contribute my skills to communicate ethical causes. It has been a joy to create graphic illustrations for children's brands and toys.

Aarin.Stewart@yahoo.com

Dear Charlotte,
AMAZING like the sea,
be all that you can be!
Little kids can do BIG things.

♡
Laura Knight